Science
1-2

Written by
Marilyn Marks

Editor: Carla Hamaguchi
Illustrator: Jenny Campbell
Designer/Production: Moonhee Pak/Mary Gagné
Cover Designer: Barbara Peterson
Art Director: Tom Cochrane
Project Director: Carolea Williams

Table of Contents

PHYSICAL SCIENCE

Introduction

Each book in the *Power Practice*™ series contains over 100 ready-to-use activity pages to provide students with skill practice. The fun activities can be used to supplement and enhance what you are teaching in your classroom. Give an activity page to students as independent class work, or send the pages home as homework to reinforce skills taught in class. An answer key is provided for quick reference.

The practical and creative activities in the science series provide the perfect way to help students develop the scientific process skills of observing, sorting, classifying, comparing, and analyzing.

Science 1–2 provides activities that illustrate and explain concepts in life science, earth science, and physical science, and the topics covered correlate with current science standards. Use the reproducible activity pages to enrich students' study of these key topics:

- habitats
- plants
- animals
- weather and seasons
- simple machines
- matter
- sound
- astronomy
- rocks and soil
- magnets

Use these ready-to-go activities to "recharge" skill review and give students the power to succeed!

Animal Homes

Habitats

Animals live in many places. Some live in trees. Some live under the ground. Other animals live in the water. Many animals build a home. Other animals find a place to call home.

Look at the picture. Write the number of each animal in the box that shows where it usually lives.

Life under the Ground

Habitats

Many animals make their home under the ground. Some underground animals have claws for digging a tunnel or a burrow. Others find a hole already made. Underground homes are a safe and warm place to raise a family.

Look at each picture. Circle all of the animals that can live under the ground.

Ant

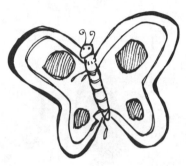

Butterfly

Some Rabbits

Robin

Mole

Some Snakes

Earthworm

Snail

Prairie Dog

Name _____   Date _____

Life in a Tree

Habitats

> You might be surprised to discover all the animals that can live in a tree. They can hide under the leaves or between the branches. Some birds build nests in the branches. Other animals live in holes in the tree. A tree can be home to many animals.

Look at the picture of the tree. Read each statement. Write **T** if the statement is true or **F** if it is false.

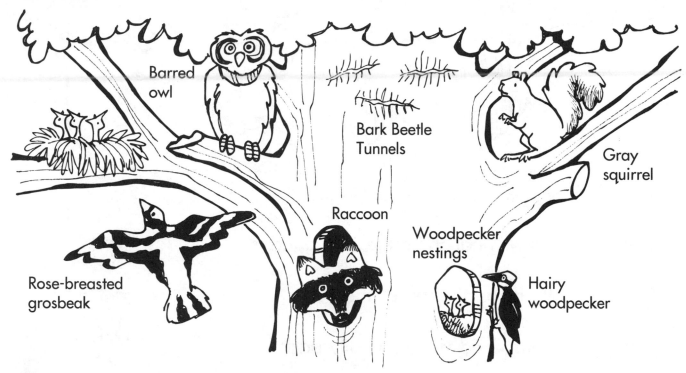

Barred owl

Bark Beetle Tunnels

Gray squirrel

Raccoon

Woodpecker nestings

Rose-breasted grosbeak

Hairy woodpecker

1 _____ Raccoons build a nest in the tree branches.

2 _____ Bark beetles dig tunnels under the tree bark.

3 _____ Woodpecker babies live in a nest inside a tree.

4 _____ The owl digs a hole in the side of the tree to make a home.

5 _____ Trees can be a good place for an animal to hide.

6 _____ Squirrels live among the tree branches or in a hole in the tree.

Life in a Pond

Habitats

A **pond** is a small body of fresh water. It is surrounded by land on all sides. Plants grow along the edges. Plants can grow on the bottom of a pond if the water is not too deep. A pond is a good home for plants and animals.

Write the letter of the picture that matches each description.

1 _____ grows near the edge of a pond

2 _____ floats on the top of the water

3 _____ swims and sits on the lily pads

4 _____ swims under the water

5 _____ bird that lives in a pond

6 _____ hard-shelled animal (reptile) that lives in a pond

A.

B.

C.

D.

E.

F.

Life in the Ocean

Habitats

Oceans cover three-fourths of the earth. They are filled with salt water. Oceans are home to many types of seaweed. All sizes of fish swim in the water. Sea-shelled animals, crabs, and whales live there, too.

What's hiding in the ocean water? Color all of the letters of the word **OCEAN** in green. Color all of the other letters blue.

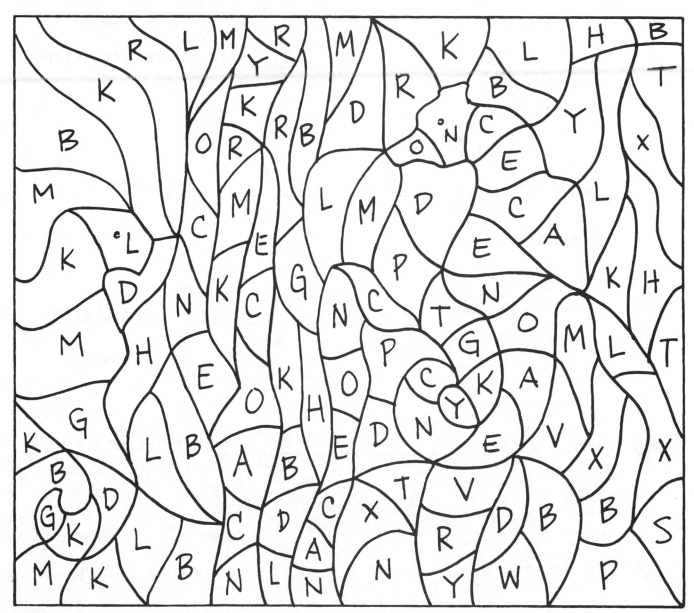

I found _____ hiding in the water.

Name _____   Date _____

Life in a Forest

Habitats

> **Forests** are places where lots of trees grow. Many forests are found in the mountains. The animals get ready for winter, when snow will cover the ground. Some store food. Others grow thick fur. Some animals leave when winter comes. They return in the spring. All of these animals call the forest home.

Write the name of the forest animal to complete each sentence.

1 A _____ sleeps, or hibernates, in the winter.

2 Many _____ fly south for the winter.

3 The _____ gathers and stores nuts for the winter.

4 The _____ grows thicker fur in winter.

5 The _____ sometimes changes the color of its fur for winter.

Animal Pets

Habitats

Animals can live in homes where people live, too. We call these animals "pets." Some stay inside. Other animals live outside in a backyard. Pets are nice friends for people.

Look at the house. Draw the pets that live in your house or draw a pet you would like to have. Be sure to draw any special cage or home each animal lives in.

I like pets because

_____

_____.

Name _____   Date _____

Plant Parts

Plants

> Plants come in all shapes and sizes. Most plants have roots, stems, leaves, and flowers. Each part of the plant has a special job to do. The soil gives the plant a place to grow. All of the parts of a plant work together to help it grow.

Look at the picture of the plant. Use the words from the box to label the parts.

stem	roots	flower	leaf	soil

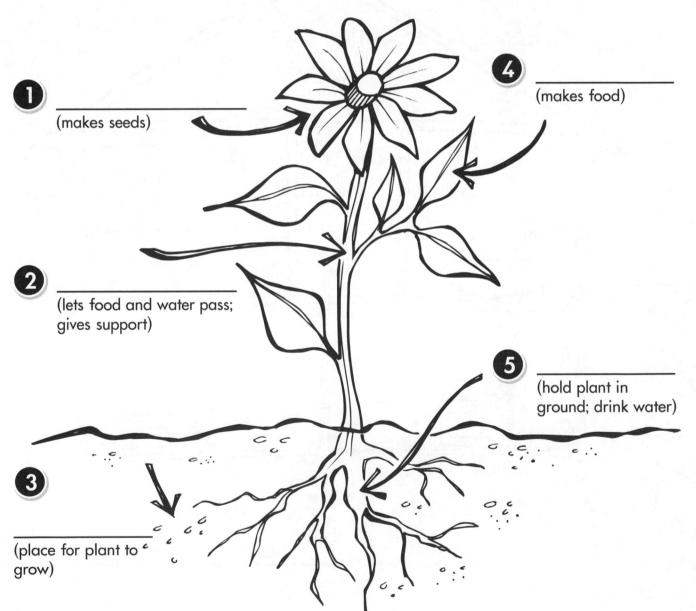

1 _____
(makes seeds)

4 _____
(makes food)

2 _____
(lets food and water pass;
gives support)

5 _____
(hold plant in
ground; drink water)

3 _____
(place for plant to
grow)

Plant Roots

Plants

Plant roots usually grow under the ground. Roots hold the plant in place. They take in water and minerals for the plant. Some plants have one big root. Others have lots of small roots. Some roots store food in them.

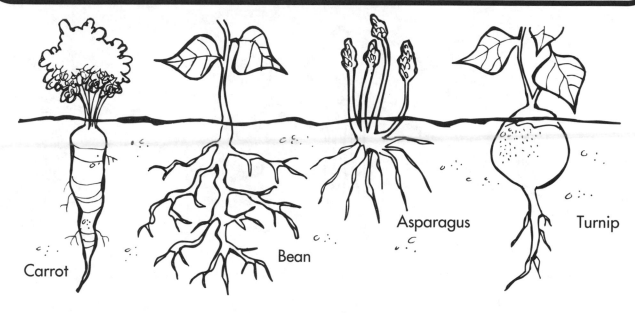

Carrot   Bean   Asparagus   Turnip

Use the words in the box to complete the sentences.

food	carrot	hold	ground	bean	water	minerals

1 Most roots grow under the _____.

2 Some plants store _____ in their roots.

3 Roots take in _____ and _____ from the soil.

4 A _____ has one big root.

5 Roots _____ the plant in the ground.

6 The _____ plant has lots of small roots.

Name _____ Date _____

Plant Stems

Plants

Stems help hold a plant up. They have special tubes inside that carry food and water to the plant. Some plant stems are thin, while others are fat. The trunk of a tree is a stem, too. Many vines have stems that cling to walls so the vines can climb.

| Onion | Daisy | Celery | Tree | Vine |

Use the words in the box to complete the sentences.

| onion | celery | tree | vines | tubes | daisy |

1 A _____ has a thin stem and a _____ has a fat stem.

2 The crunchiness of _____ comes from the special

_____ that carry food and water in the plant.

3 The stem of an _____ is a bulb that grows under the ground.

4 Many _____ have stems that can cling and climb up a wall.

Plant Leaves

Plants

Plant leaves are very busy. They breathe air in and out. Leaves use the sun's energy to help them make food for the plant. Leaves come in all shapes and sizes.

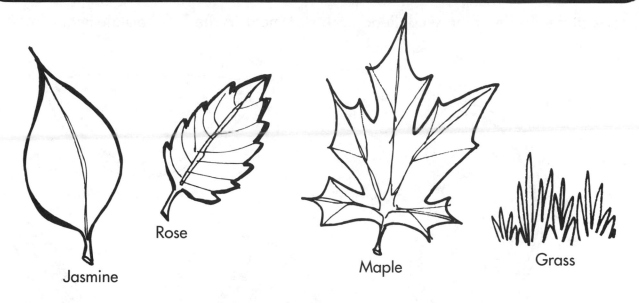

Jasmine

Rose

Maple

Grass

Use the words in the box to complete the sentences.

rose	grass	sun	jasmine	air	maple

1 Plant leaves use the energy from the _____ to help them make food.

2 Leaves breathe _____ in and out.

3 The _____ has leaves that are all smooth on the edges.

4 The _____ has leaves that have jagged edges.

5 The _____ tree has big leaves that are pointy in places.

6 _____ has leaves that are long and thin.

Name _____ Date _____

Plant Seeds

Plants

> Seeds are very important. They have a baby plant inside. If you plant a seed, a new plant will grow. Some plants make big seeds. Others make tiny seeds. Peas and beans have several seeds in a pod.

Look at the inside of the seed. Read each statement. Write **T** if the statement is true or **F** if it is false.

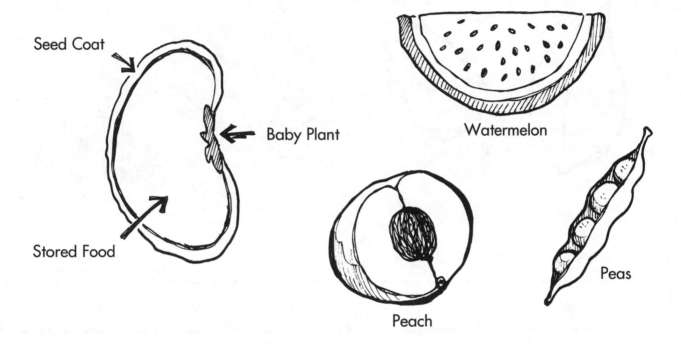

Seed Coat

Baby Plant

Stored Food

Watermelon

Peach

Peas

1 _____ The outside of the seed is covered by a seed coat.

2 _____ The baby plant takes up most of the space inside the seed.

3 _____ A seed has stored food inside.

4 _____ A peach has two tiny seeds.

5 _____ Peas and beans have several seeds in a pod.

6 _____ A watermelon makes lots of seeds.

Science • 1–2 © 2005 Creative Teaching Press

Name _____ Date _____

Plants Make Flowers

Plants

Flowers look pretty and smell nice. But that is not why plants make them. Flowers are important because it is their job to make seeds. Seeds are how most plants reproduce. The center of the flower makes the seeds.

Find names of the flowers in the word search. The words go across, down, and backwards.

Z	R	O	S	E	A	B	N	O
C	A	R	N	A	T	I	O	N
B	S	A	V	C	D	Y	D	E
R	G	L	I	L	A	B	S	P
V	F	H	X	O	I	J	I	T
P	O	P	P	Y	S	K	R	U
W	H	F	M	A	Y	L	I	L
I	J	L	O	W	X	O	P	I
X	P	E	T	U	N	I	A	P
U	A	U	E	U	T	C	I	L
K	N	L	E	R	D	E	Z	T
A	S	T	E	R	M	O	A	B
L	Y	U	T	N	A	K	C	R

rose

daisy

petunia

lily

poppy

pansy

aster

carnation

iris

tulip

Science • 1–2 © 2005 Creative Teaching Press

How Plants Grow

Plants

Most plants sprout from seeds. Plants need water and sunlight in order to grow. Tiny leaves appear above the soil. Soon, more leaves appear on the stem. Then a plant can make a flower. If it is too hot or too cold, the plant may die.

Look at the first picture in each row. Color the picture that shows what will happen next.

Science • 1–2 © 2005 Creative Teaching Press

Plant Parts We Eat

Plants

> The food that plants make can be stored in any part of the plant. We can eat roots, stems, leaves, flowers, fruits, or seeds. When we eat plants we are eating the food they have made. Many plants are good to eat.

Asparagus

Carrot

Corn

Spinach

Peanut

Watermelon

Lettuce

Celery

Pear

Broccoli

Beet

Cauliflower

Write the name of the plant next to the part we eat.

Roots _____ _____   Stems _____ _____

Leaves _____ _____   Flowers _____ _____

Fruits _____ _____   Seeds _____ _____

Name _____   Date _____

Tree Families

Plants

There are two main types of trees. Some are in the **evergreen** family. They stay green all year round. Other trees are in the **hardwood** family. These trees often lose their leaves in the winter.

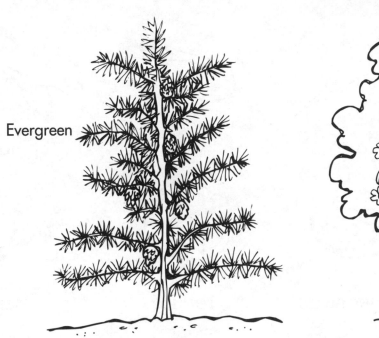

Evergreen

Hardwood

Read each statement. Write an **E** if the sentence is about evergreen trees or **H** if the sentence is about hardwood trees.

1 _____ These trees make some kind of cone.

2 _____ These trees often lose their leaves in the winter.

3 _____ These trees stay green all year long.

4 _____ These trees have thin, needle-like leaves.

5 _____ These trees make flowers.

6 _____ These trees are used for Christmas trees.

Science • 1–2 © 2005 Creative Teaching Press

Name _____ Date _____

Trees Are Useful

Plants

Trees are very useful. They make the air cleaner. They give us shade on a hot day. Some trees give us fruits or nuts to eat. We use the wood from trees to make many things.

Color all the pictures that show things we get from trees or that are made from trees.

Plastic Bag

Pencil

Drinking Glass

Newspaper

Wooden Chair

Coat

Aluminum

Cardboard Box

Apple

Name _____ Date _____

My Eyes

Fives Senses and Nutrition

Your eyes let you see. Each part of your eye has a special job. Inside your eye is a lens that lets you see things in focus. It is important to take good care of your eyes.

Look at the pictures of the parts of the eye. Use the words in the box to complete the sentences.

| eyelashes | tears | pupil | iris | white part | lens |

1. Your _____ keep dust out of your eyes.

2. The _____, or colored part, adjusts the amount of light going into the eye.

3. The _____ is a hole that lets light enter the eye.

4. The _____ _____ doesn't see; it protects the inside of the eye.

5. The _____ is inside your eye. It brings the light to a focus.

6. _____ wash the eye to keep it clean.

My Ears

Five Senses and Nutrition

Your ears let you hear. Sound is guided into the ear. Sound waves make the eardrum wiggle, or vibrate. The vibrations are passed deeper into your ear. The ear sends these sound messages to your brain. Then you can hear them.

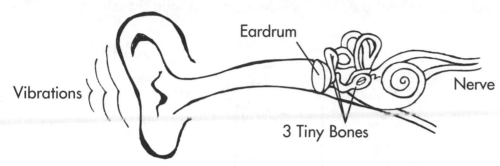

Look at the pictures. Circle all of the things that you can hear with your ears.

Name _____   Date _____

How Does It Taste?

Five Senses and Nutrition

Your tongue lets you taste the foods you eat. The tongue can only taste four flavors: bitter, sweet, sour, and salty. The center of the tongue lets you feel if the food is hot, cold, lumpy, or sticky. Foods do not taste the same to everyone.

Draw a line from each picture to the part of the tongue that would taste it.

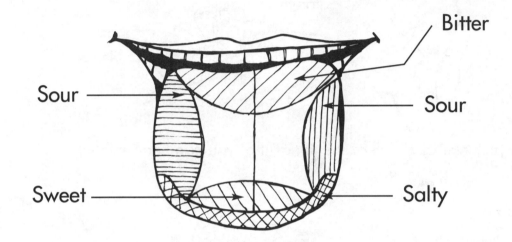

Bitter

Sour ——————   —————— Sour

Sweet ——————   —————— Salty

Name _____   Date _____

How Does It Smell?

Five Senses and Nutrition

> Your nose can smell many things. You do not even have to be in the same room to smell something. We really smell our food more than we taste it. When you have a cold and your nose is stopped up you cannot taste food very well.

Circle the items that smell good. Underline the items that smell bad.

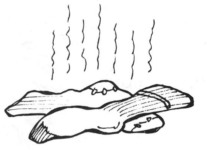

Sense of Touch

Five Senses and Nutrition

Your skin lets you know how things feel when you touch them. Nerves in the skin tell your brain if something is rough or smooth, hot or cold, or hard or soft. Your skin also tells you if something hurts.

Each word tells how something feels. Color the picture in the row that matches the word.

1 Pain

2 Smooth

3 Cold

4 Hard

5 Soft

Name _____ Date _____

Healthy Eating

Five Senses and Nutrition

It is important to eat the right foods if you want to be healthy. The food pyramid is a guide to healthy eating. You should try to eat foods from all of the groups except "extras" every day. Healthy foods will give you all the nutrients you need.

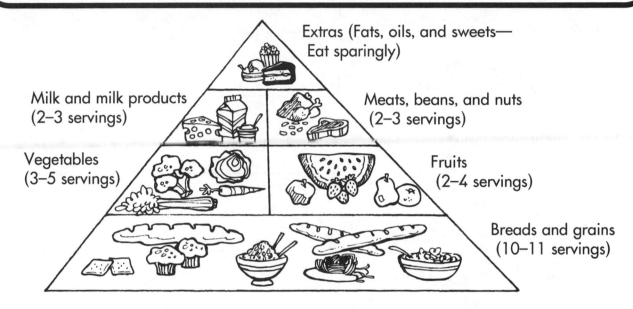

Extras (Fats, oils, and sweets— Eat sparingly)

Milk and milk products (2–3 servings)

Meats, beans, and nuts (2–3 servings)

Vegetables (3–5 servings)

Fruits (2–4 servings)

Breads and grains (10–11 servings)

Use the information in the food pyramid to complete the sentences.

1 Celery and spinach belong to the _____ group.

2 You should try to eat _____ servings of milk and milk products every day.

3 Fish and chicken belong to the _____ group.

4 You should try to eat 2–4 servings from the _____ group each day.

5 Pasta and crackers belong to the _____ group.

6 Donuts, cookies, and candy belong to the _____ group.

Science • 1–2 © 2005 Creative Teaching Press

Name _____ Date _____

Fruits and Vegetables

Five Senses and Nutrition

> **Fruits** are made by the flower of a plant. Fruits have seeds in them. Not all fruits taste sweet. **Vegetables** can be any other part of a plant. They can be a root, a stem, or a leaf. Fruits and vegetables give us lots of vitamins and minerals.

Write **fruit** or **vegetable** to label each picture.

1   is a _____.

2  is a _____.

3   is a _____.

4  are a _____.

5  is a _____.

6  are a _____.

7  is a _____.

8  is a _____.

9 is a _____.

Name _____ Date _____

Body Word Scramble

Five Senses and Nutrition

Do you know the parts of your body? Unscramble the words and complete the sentences.

heart	brain	eyes	ears	lungs
tongue	bones	skin	nose	

1 SEBNO = _____, which form my skeleton.

2 TREHA = _____, which pumps blood through my body.

3 ESON = _____, which I use to smell.

4 BNIAR = _____, which receives messages from all over my body.

5 IKSN = _____, which covers the outside of my body.

6 UNLGS = _____, which I use for breathing.

7 YEES = _____, which I use to see.

8 SARE = _____, which I use to hear.

9 EUGTNO = _____, which I use for tasting.

Insects

Animals

> **Insects** are small animals without any bones. Insects have six legs and three parts to their body. Most insects have wings. Many have feelers, or antennae, on their head. There are more insects on earth than any other kind of animal.

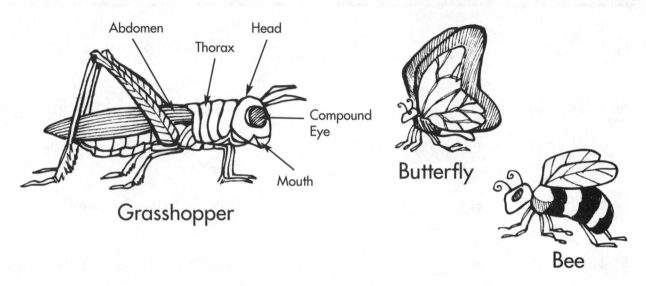

Abdomen   Thorax   Head

Compound Eye

Mouth

Grasshopper

Butterfly

Bee

Look at the pictures. Read each statement. Write **T** if the statement is true or **F** if it is false.

1 _____ Insects are small animals.

2 _____ An insect's legs are attached to its abdomen.

3 _____ Many insects have feelers, or antennae, on their head.

4 _____ Insects have a skeleton made of bones.

5 _____ Insect bodies are divided into four parts.

6 _____ There are more insects on earth than any other kind of animal.

7 _____ Most insects have wings for flying.

8 _____ Many insects have very large eyes, called compound eyes.

Name _____ Date _____

Insect Metamorphosis

Animals

Insects hatch from eggs. Insect babies do not look like their parents. Insects go through several stages before they become adults. This process of change is called **metamorphosis.**

Incomplete metamorphosis

Grasshopper egg   nymph   nymph  adult

Complete metamorphosis

Ant egg   larva  pupa  adult

Use the words in the box to complete the sentences.

eggs   nymphs   adult   larva   pupa   metamorphosis

1 Insects hatch from _____.

2 Young insects that look more like their parents are called _____.

3 The process of changing into an adult insect is called _____.

4 A caterpillar would be in the _____ stage of growth.

5 When an insect wraps itself up to finish changing, it is called the _____.

6 In the final stage of an insect's growth, it becomes an _____.

Name _____ Date _____

Amphibians

Animals

> **Amphibians** are animals that can live on the land and in the water. They look like tadpoles when they are young. When they grow up, most amphibians develop lungs and then live on land where they breathe air.

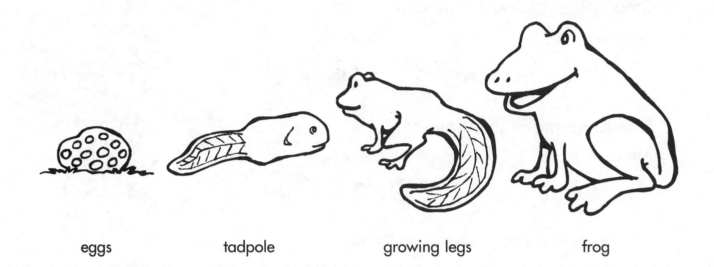

| eggs | tadpole | growing legs | frog |

Use the words in the box to complete the sentences.

| gills | eggs | tadpoles | frogs | legs | lungs |

A mother frog lays her _____ in the water. The eggs hatch

1

into _____, which look like little fish, but they are not

2

fish. Tadpoles breathe under the water with _____.

3

Later, they will grow four _____ and also have

4

_____. Now they are called _____. Frogs

5   6

live on the land and in the water.

Science Enrichment • 1–2 © 2005 Creative Teaching Press

Name _____ Date _____

Reptiles

Animals

Reptiles hatch from eggs. Their eggs are not as hard as a chicken's egg. Reptile babies look like their parents, only smaller. They breathe air just like we do. They have lungs, too.

Circle all of the animals that are reptiles.

Earthworm

Frog

Lizard

Tadpole

Trout

Alligator

Snake

Snail

Turtle

Name _____ Date _____

Fish

Animals

Fish must live in water. It can be the fresh water in a river or lake. It can be the salt water in the ocean. Fish breathe under the water with gills. Fish come in all shapes and sizes.

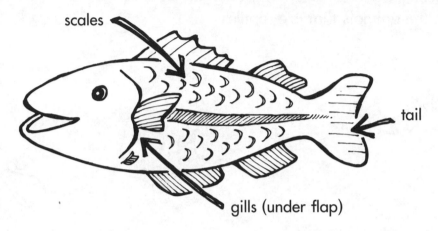

scales

tail

gills (under flap)

Look at the picture. Read each statement. Write **T** if the statement is true or **F** if it is false.

1 _____ Most fish have a skeleton made of bones.

2 _____ Fish are covered with wet scales.

3 _____ Most fish lay eggs.

4 _____ Fish have tails.

5 _____ Fish breathe with gills.

6 _____ Sharks, tuna, and trout are all fish.

Science • 1–2 © 2005 Creative Teaching Press

Name _____ Date _____

Birds

Animals

> **Birds** are the only animals covered with feathers. The feathers keep birds warm and dry. Most birds can fly. Birds lay hard-shelled eggs. Birds build a nest to hold their eggs.

Robin

Flamingo

Oriole

Woodpecker

Barn Swallow

Look at all the bird nests. Use the words in the box to complete the sentences.

mud	hanging	round	barn	hole

1 The flamingo uses _____ to build its nest in the water.

2 The woodpecker builds its nest in a _____ in a tree.

3 The robin builds a _____ nest between the branches of a tree.

4 The barn swallow usually builds its nest in the corner of a _____.

5 The oriole builds a _____ nest near the ends of a branch.

Mammals

Animals

Mammals are animals that are covered with hair or fur. Their babies are born alive. The mother nurses the babies with milk she makes inside her body. Mammals spend a lot of time taking care of their babies.

Follow the directions to mark the pictures of the mammals.

1 Circle the mammal that lives in the ocean.

2 Underline the mammal that hops.

3 Draw an X on the mammal that lives on a farm.

4 Color the mammal that is usually a pet yellow.

5 Draw a box around the mammal that lives in the jungle.

6 Color the mammal that can fly brown.

What's on the Outside of an Animal's Body?

Animals

> Animals have different body coverings. Some animals have a shell to protect them. Some have moist skin. Other animals are covered with scales. Birds have feathers. Mammals are covered with hair or fur.

Can you tell what the animals are covered with? Follow the directions to mark the pictures.

1 Underline the animals covered with feathers.

2 Circle the animals covered with moist skin.

3 Color the animals covered with hair or fur.

4 Draw a box around the animals covered with scales.

5 Draw an X on the animals covered by a shell.

Colorful Animals

Animals

There are many animals in this picture. Follow the directions to color the picture.

Color the mammals BLUE.   Color the reptiles RED.
Color the birds GREEN.   Color the insects PURPLE.
Color the fish YELLOW.   Color the amphibians ORANGE.

What Animals Eat

Animals

Sometimes you can tell by looking at an animal what it likes to eat. Some animals eat plants. Some animals have sharp teeth for eating other animals. Look at an animal's teeth or its beak to determine what it might eat.

Look at the pictures. Read each statement. Write **T** if the statement is true or **F** if it is false.

1 _____ Rabbits like to eat plants.

2 _____ Lions and tigers like to eat meat from other animals.

3 _____ Snakes like to eat plants.

4 _____ Lots of birds eat plants and animals.

5 _____ Cows like to eat plants.

6 _____ Sharks like to eat plants.

Name _____ Date _____

How Animals Move

Animals

Some animals crawl or slither. Others hop or jump. Some swim. Some animals can fly. Animals use legs, feet, fins, or wings to move. Each animal has its own way of getting around.

Look at the pictures of the animals. Write the name of the animal to complete each sentence.

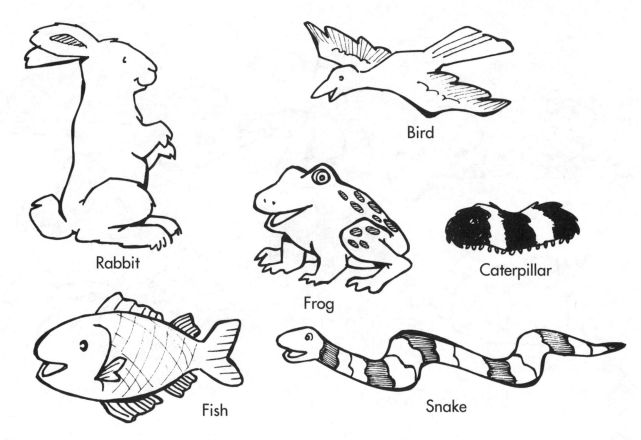

Rabbit

Bird

Frog

Caterpillar

Fish

Snake

1 A _____ can swim.

2 A _____ can hop or jump.

3 A _____ can fly.

4 A _____ slithers from place to place.

5 A _____ crawls slowly.

Animals of Long Ago

Dinosaurs

Millions of years ago, dinosaurs roamed the earth. They are all gone now. Some modern animals have some of the same features that dinosaurs had. These features help the animals to survive.

Match each dinosaur to the modern animal that resembles it.

 1 ____ Pachecephalosaursus

 **a.** Giraffe

 2 ____ Pteranodon

b. Bighorn Sheep

 3 ____ Triceratops

c. Albatross

 4 ____ Apatosaurus

d. Rhinoceros

Dinosaur Lunch

Dinosaurs

Some dinosaurs ate plants. Others were meat-eaters. They ate other animals. We find fossils that give us clues to what the dinosaurs were like.

Look at the pictures. Read each statement. Write **T** if the statement is true or **F** if it is false.

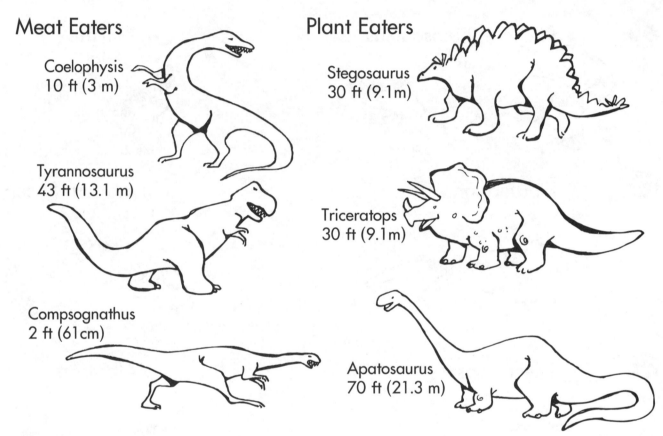

Meat Eaters

Coelophysis
10 ft (3 m)

Tyrannosaurus
43 ft (13.1 m)

Compsognathus
2 ft (61cm)

Plant Eaters

Stegosaurus
30 ft (9.1m)

Triceratops
30 ft (9.1m)

Apatosaurus
70 ft (21.3 m)

1 _____ All of the plant-eating dinosaurs had small heads.

2 _____ The meat-eating dinosaurs were all very big.

3 _____ Meat-eating dinosaurs had sharp teeth.

4 _____ Dinosaurs probably had to eat a lot of food.

5 _____ Most meat-eating dinosaurs could stand up on their back legs.

Science • 1–2 © 2005 Creative Teaching Press

Dinosaur Footprints

Dinosaurs

We find dinosaur bones and footprints in rocks. These are called **fossils**. The dinosaur's footprints tell us about the size of the dinosaur. If the footprints are far apart, the dinosaur moved fast.

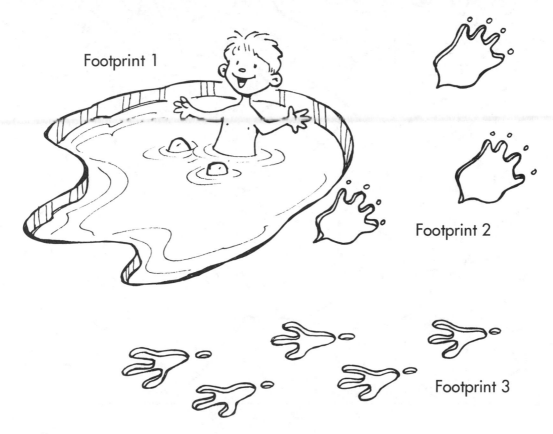

Footprint 1

Footprint 2

Footprint 3

Write the number of the footprint that answers each question.

1 _____ Which dinosaur footprint is very large?

2 _____ Which footprint shows a dinosaur that walked slowly?

3 _____ Which footprint shows a dinosaur that walked fast?

4 _____ Which footprint tells us the dinosaur had four toes?

5 _____ Which footprint tells us the dinosaur had three toes?

Dinosaur Puzzle

Dinosaurs

Color all of the letters of the word **DINOSAUR** brown. Color all the other letters green.
Which dinosaur did you find?

Triceratops

Tyrannosaurus

Stegosaurus

The dinosaur in the puzzle is a _____.

Science • 1–2 © 2005 Creative Teaching Press

Name _____ Date _____

What Is Soil?

Rocks and Soil

Soil is the top of the ground. You may call it dirt. You can find it in a garden. Soil is under the grass, too. Soil is made of many things.

Use the words in the box to complete the sentences.

sand	plants	soil	animals	water	rocks

Wind and _____ make _____
1   2

crumble into _____. _____ and
3   4

 _____ die and decay and turn into small bits called
5

humus. Sand mixed with the humus makes good  _____.
6

What Is a Rock?

Rocks and Soil

Rocks are small pieces of the earth's surface. You can see some rocks on top of the ground. Many rocks are hidden under the ground. Some rocks are big and heavy. Others are small pebbles.

Follow the directions to mark the pictures.

1 Circle the rocks that are dark colored.

2 Underline the rocks that are speckled.

3 Put a ✔ by the rocks that would feel smooth to touch.

4 Draw a box around the rocks that would feel rough to touch.

Name _____ Date _____

Why Don't Rocks Last Forever?

Rocks and Soil

Rocks last for a very long time. But they do not last forever. Rocks crack, break, and wear away. This is called **weathering**. If the pieces are carried away to a new place, then we call it **erosion**.

What changed the land in each picture? Use the words in the box to answer the question.

wind	water	ice	earthquake

1 Changed by _____

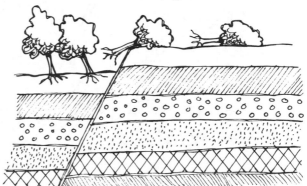

2 Changed by _____

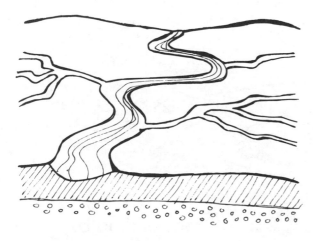

3 Changed by _____

4 Changed by _____

Name _____ Date _____

What Do People Do with Rocks?

Rocks and Soil

Rocks are very useful. They can be used for building houses and roads. Some rocks are used to build dams that hold water. Rocks can be used for decoration, too.

Use the words in the box to complete each phrase.

house	road	dam	decoration

1 Used for building a

_____

2 Used for building a

_____

3 Used for

_____

4 Used for building a

_____

Rocks Have Hidden Treasures

Rocks and Soil

Rocks can have useful things hidden inside them. Some rocks contain metals, like iron or copper. We use the metal to make pots, pennies, and cans. We dig up lots of these useful rocks every year.

Color all the pictures that show something made from rocks.

Some Rocks Are Pretty

Rocks and Soil

> Some rocks are very pretty. They can be cut and polished until they are shiny. We make jewelry out of them. Rocks or minerals used for jewelry are called **gems**.

Look at the pictures. Read each statement. Write **T** if the statement is true or **F** if it is false.

Gold Jewelry

Emerald
May Birthstone

Diamond
April Birthstone

Amethyst
February Birthstone

Ruby
July Birthstone

Sapphire
September
Birthstone

Turquoise
December Birthstone

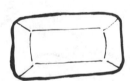

Garnet
January Birthstone

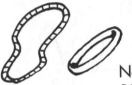

Topaz
November
Birthstone

1 _____ Gold found in rocks is used for making jewelry.

2 _____ If you were born in February, the diamond is your birthstone.

3 _____ Pretty rocks and minerals used for jewelry are called gems.

4 _____ Topaz is the birthstone for November.

5 _____ Rocks can be cut and polished until they are shiny and pretty.

6 _____ Ruby is the birthstone for July.

Rocks from Long Ago

Rocks and Soil

Scientists study rocks to find out what the earth was like many years ago. The scientists use special tools to discover the age of the rocks. Some rocks found near the surface can be very old. Other old rocks are buried deep in the ground.

Use the words in the box to complete the sentences.

age	earth	dig	tools	deep

1 Scientists study rocks to find out what the _____ was like long ago.

2 Many old rocks are buried _____ under the ground.

3 Scientists can discover the _____ of the rock.

4 Scientists use special _____ to help them study rocks.

5 Usually, we have to _____ in the ground to uncover rocks.

Over Hill and Dale—Landforms

Rocks and Soil

The surface of the earth is not all smooth. There are places where mountains stick up. There are lower valleys. Some areas are flat land, called **plains**. The earth has many different landforms.

Use the words in the box to complete each sentence.

mountain	hill	valley	plain	cliff	canyon

1 This is a _____

2 This is a _____

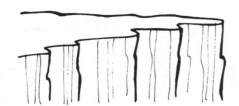

3 This is a _____

4 This is a _____

5 This is a _____

6 This is a _____

Science Enrichment • 1–2 © 2005 Creative Teaching Press

Name _____ Date _____

Earth Crossword Puzzle

Rocks and Soil

Complete the crossword puzzle. Use the words in the box for help.

mountain	rocks	mud	water
soil	sand	island	hill

Across

1. land much higher than a hill
2. large and small stony pieces found on earth's surface
3. another name for dirt

Down

1. wet soil or earth
3. rocks wear down and crumble into this
4. area of land with water all around it
5. wind and _____ cause weathering and erosion
6. raised land, but smaller than a mountain

Name _____   Date _____

Earth's Natural Resources

Natural Resources

The sun shines on the earth and keeps us warm. The sun helps plants to grow. The air, water, and land give us things we use every day. We call all of these things **natural resources**.

Put a ✔ in the boxes that show things we get from nature. These are earth's natural resources.

1 Air and Sun

2 Land
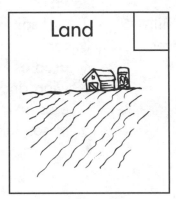

3 Houses

4 Trees

5 TV
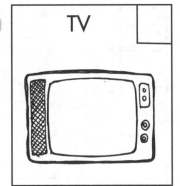

6 Water

7 Toys

8 Ocean

9 Oil

Science • 1–2 © 2005 Creative Teaching Press

What Wastes Natural Resources?

Natural Resources

When you waste water or paper you use up some of the earth's resources. We should try to keep the earth clean. You can help save energy by turning off lights, recycling paper, and turning off water faucets tightly.

Draw an **X** through the pictures that show someone wasting natural resources.

What Is Smog?

Natural Resources

The fuel used in our cars and in factories can make the air dirty. Dirty air creates smog. Smog can make the sky look brown. Smog can hurt your eyes. Breathing smog is not healthy.

Look at the picture. Read each statement. Write **T** if the statement is true or **F** if it is false.

1 _____ Smog is dirty air.

2 _____ Lots of cars driving on the streets create smog.

3 _____ Breathing smog does not hurt you.

4 _____ Some factories produce smog.

5 _____ There is nothing we can do to prevent smog.

6 _____ The wind can help to blow smog away.

Name _____   Date _____

How We Use Water

Natural Resources

We all use water every day. We drink it, cook with it, and wash with it. All living things need water to stay alive. Many people work on boats that travel across the ocean. Water is used in many ways.

Under each picture write how water is being used. You will use the words in the box more than one time.

fun	work	daily living

1 _____

2 _____

3 _____

4 _____

5 _____

6 _____

7 _____

8 _____

9 _____

Help Save Our Water

Natural Resources

Water is one of our most important natural resources. All the water on the earth gets recycled. We need to be careful not to waste water. You can help your family use water wisely.

Find and circle four ways that water is being wasted in this picture.

Saving Energy at Home

Natural Resources

When we waste energy we are wasting our natural resources. We use natural resources to make electricity. We use natural gas from the earth for cooking and for heating our homes. It also heats water for washing and bathing.

Can you find five ways that energy is being wasted? Color them.

What Saves Paper?

Natural Resources

Paper is made from the wood we get from trees. When you waste paper you are wasting trees. Think about what you can do to save paper. This will save one of our natural resources.

Put a ✔ by the things that will help us save paper.

1 _____ Writing on both sides of a page of paper

2 _____ Using paper drinking cups that we can throw away

3 _____ Using cloth towels to dry dishes

4 _____ Recycling old newspapers

5 _____ Reusing old glass jars

6 _____ Erasing our mistakes instead of starting over on a new page of paper

Name _____   Date _____

How We Use Air

Natural Resources

All living things need clean air to breathe. Air is a useful natural resource. We also use air to make things work, to dry things, and sometimes just for fun. Think about how you use air every day.

Under each picture write how air is being used. You will use the words in the box more than one time.

dry things	make things work	for fun

1 _____

2 _____

3 _____

4 _____

5 _____

6 _____

7 _____

8 _____

9 _____

Name _____ Date _____

Where on Earth Does Our Food Come From?

Natural Resources

All of our food comes from the environment. We grow plants and raise animals that give us food. We need good land for the plants to grow. Many animals that live on farms and ranches give us food.

Use the words in the box to complete each sentence.

cows   lambs   fish   trees   farms   chickens   milk

1 We get poultry and eggs from _____.

2 We get meat to eat from _____ and _____.

3 We get apples, oranges, and cherries from _____.

4 Carrots, corn, and lettuce are grown on _____.

5 When we eat tuna or trout we are eating _____.

6 Cows give us _____ to drink and to make cheese from.

Name _____ Date _____

Where Does Our Water Come From?

Natural Resources

Every time you turn on a faucet, clean water comes out. It comes from up in the mountains, from lakes and rivers, and even from under the ground. Big pipes carry water to your house. Pumping stations help to push the water along.

Look at the picture. Read each statement. Write **T** if the statement is true or **F** if it is false.

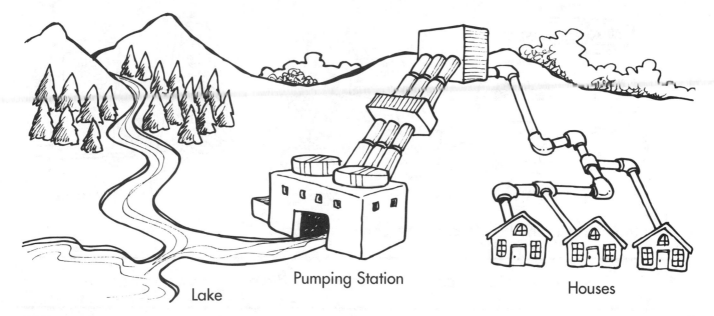

Lake   Pumping Station   Houses

1 _____ We get our drinking water from the ocean.

2 _____ Water travels to your house in pipes.

3 _____ Sometimes we find water under the ground.

4 _____ When we turn on a faucet, clean water comes out.

5 _____ Pumping stations help to move water to your house.

6 _____ Lakes and rivers give us fresh water for washing and cooking.

7 _____ When snow in the mountains melts, we can get more water.

Name _____ Date _____

Where Does Fuel Come From?

Natural Resources

There are many kinds of fuels. Some make your car run. Other fuels are used for heating and cooking. Many fuels come out of the ground. Some are made in refineries.

natural gas stove   coal   wood   oil   gasoline

Use the words in the box to complete each sentence.

wood	oil	coal	gasoline	diesel	natural gas stove

1 Early pioneers burned _____ for fuel.

2 We use a _____ for cooking and heating our homes.

3 We drill into the ground to find _____, which we use in many ways.

4 We use lots of _____ to make our cars run.

5 We dig up a black rock, called _____, which is used in power plants.

6 Lots of trucks use _____ fuel.

What Are Our Clothes Made From?

Natural Resources

Draw a line from the plant or animal to the clothing that is made from it.

Cotton Plant

Silkworm

Flax Plant

Sheep

Cows

T-shirt

Silk Scarf

Wool Sweater

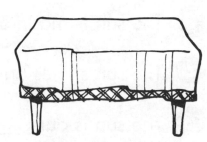
Leather Shoes

Linen Tablecloth

Name _____ Date _____

The Sun

Astronomy

> The sun is a star in the sky. A star is a ball of bright, hot gases. There are many stars in the sky, but the sun is our closest star. The sun gives us light and keeps us warm.

Use the words in the box to complete each sentence.

gases	hot	star	closest	light	bright

1 The sun is a _____ in the sky.

2 The sun looks very _____.

3 The sun is made of very hot _____.

4 The sun shines on the earth and gives us _____.

5 The sun is our _____ star.

6 If you could touch the Sun, it would feel very, very _____.

Day and Night

Astronomy

The earth turns all the way around each day. We say the earth rotates. When the sun shines on our part of the earth we have daytime. When our part of the earth is dark we have nighttime.

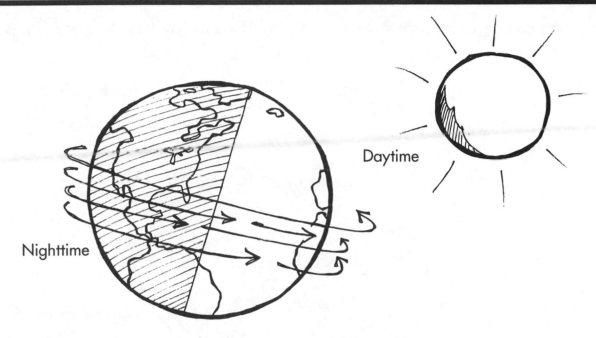

Daytime

Nighttime

Use the words in the box to complete each sentence.

twenty-four	day	night	rotates	warmer	colder

1 One day lasts for _____ hours.

2 During the day, the sun makes the earth _____.

3 At night the earth is _____.

4 Every day the earth turns around, or _____.

5 The sun shines on our part of the earth during the _____.

6 We do not see the sun during the _____.

Name _____ Date _____

The Moon

Astronomy

The moon is much smaller than the earth. The moon travels around the earth. We can see the moon at night. The surface of the moon has many different landforms.

Look at the picture. Read each statement. Write **T** if the statement is true or **F** if it is false.

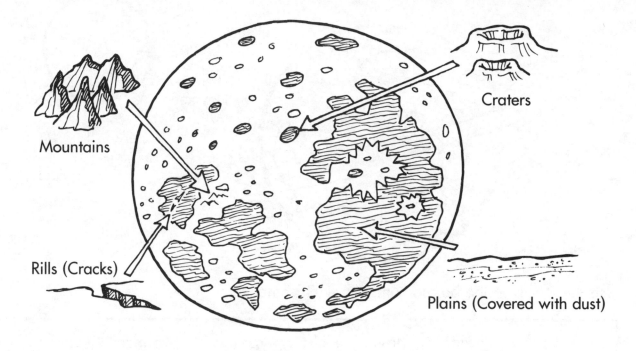

Craters

Mountains

Rills (Cracks)

Plains (Covered with dust)

1 _____ The moon is about the same size as the earth.

2 _____ Big dents or holes on the surface of the moon are called craters.

3 _____ Flat areas of the moon's surface are called rills.

4 _____ There are mountains on the moon.

5 _____ The moon travels around the earth.

6 _____ Large parts of the moon's surface are covered with dust.

Science • 1–2 © 2005 Creative Teaching Press

Starry Night

Astronomy

If you look at the sky at night, you can see many stars. Some people imagine they see pictures in the stars. Star pictures are called **constellations**. Have you ever looked for pictures in the stars?

Little Dipper or Little Bear

Big Dipper or Big Bear

Little Dog

Sirius

Big Dog

Orion the Hunter

Use the words in the box to complete each sentence.

Little	Big	Belt	dog	constellations

1 The North Star is found in the _____ Dipper.

2 The _____ Dipper is found in the Big Bear.

3 Star pictures that people imagine they see in the night sky are called
_____.

4 There are three stars close to each other in Orion's _____.

5 Near Orion is a constellation that people imagined looks like a
_____.

Name _____ Date _____

Cloudy Day

Weather and Seasons

Clouds come in many shapes and sizes. You can learn about the weather if you look at the clouds. Some clouds tell us we will have fair weather. Other clouds tell us that rain is coming.

Cumulus clouds look like fluffy heaps of cotton.

Stratus clouds look like sheets extending across the sky.

Cirrus clouds are curly, wispy clouds high in the air.

Cumulonimbus clouds are large, dark, storm clouds.

| cumulus | cirrus | stratus | cumulonimbus |

Use the words in the box to complete each sentence. Draw the missing clouds in each picture.

1 You can see these wispy, curly clouds high up in the sky. They are called _____ clouds.

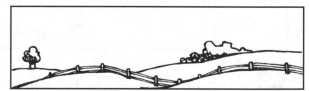

2 These giant, dark clouds tell us a storm is coming soon. They are called _____ clouds.

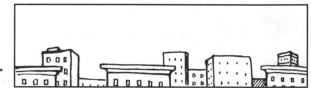

3 These white, fluffy clouds tell us we are going to have a nice day. They are called _____ clouds.

4 These clouds look like a blanket of gray over the sky. They are called _____ clouds.

Name _____ Date _____

Sunny Day

Weather and Seasons

Sometimes there are no clouds in the sky at all. Other times there may be a few clouds. Clouds form when the air can't hold any more moisture. Sunny days can be warm or cool.

Look at the picture. Read each statement. Write **T** if the statement is true or **F** if it is false.

1 _____ We will have sunny weather if there are no clouds.

2 _____ It can be a sunny day even if the weather feels colder.

3 _____ The sun is always hidden when we have clouds in the sky.

4 _____ Moisture in the air helps to form clouds.

5 _____ We enjoy being outside on sunny days.

Name _____   Date _____

Is It Going to Rain?

Weather and Seasons

The air is like a sponge. It can soak up moisture. Clouds form from this moisture. When the clouds are full of water we have a chance of rain. All the water in the clouds makes them look dark.

Use the words in the box to complete each sentence.

moisture	air	clouds	rain	dark

1 The air can soak up _____.

2 When clouds are full of water they look _____.

3 When puddles of water dry up the water goes up into the _____.

4 The moisture in the air forms _____.

5 When the clouds cannot hold any more water it might _____.

Name _____   Date _____

What's the Temperature?

Weather and Seasons

The sun helps give us our weather. The sun heats the air. A **thermometer** is used to measure the temperature of the air. That tells us how hot or cold it is. Can you read a thermometer?

A
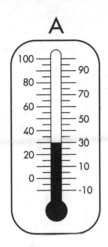

B
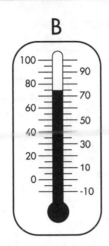

C

Decide which thermometer shows the weather described in the sentence. Write **A**, **B**, or **C** on the line.

1 _____ It is too hot to go out and play very much. Stay inside today.

2 _____ This feels like a nice day. Let's go outside and play.

3 _____ It is very cold today. Most people want to stay inside.

4 _____ Many people try to go to the beach to cool off in this weather.

5 _____ Turn the heater on in the car. There might be snow on the ground.

Name _____ Date _____

The Four Seasons

Weather and Seasons

We have four seasons: autumn, winter, spring, and summer. Each season brings us different weather. It is colder in the winter and warmer in the summer. Plants and animals adjust to changes in the seasons.

Write the name of the season under each picture.

1 _____ **2** _____ **3** _____ **4** _____

5 _____ **6** _____ **7** _____ **8** _____

Name _____ Date _____

What's Falling Out of the Sky—Precipitation

Weather and Seasons

When the clouds cannot hold any more water we get precipitation. What falls out of the sky is usually rain. There are other forms of precipitation, too. Sometimes we get sleet, or hail, or snow.

Draw a line from the picture on the left to the words that describe it on the right.

1 Snow

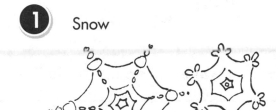

Soft crystals or flakes of ice formed in clouds when the temperature falls below freezing.

2 Rain

Frozen or partly frozen rain.

3 Hail

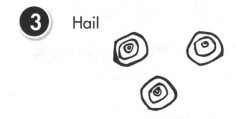

Drops of water that fall to the ground.

4 Sleet

Small round pieces of ice that fall like rain. They form during summer thunderstorms.

Weather Word Scramble

Weather and Seasons

There are lots of ways to describe the weather. It can be cold, hot, nice, foggy, cloudy, windy, rainy, snowy, or even stormy. People always talk about the weather.

| thunder | lightning | rain | snow | fog | wind | clouds | hail |

Unscramble the words and complete the sentences. Use the word box if you need help.

1 GFO is _____, which is really a cloud close to the ground.

2 LGHITNIGN is _____, a flash of light in the sky during a storm.

3 HUDERTN is _____, the noise you hear after you see lightning.

4 AIHL is _____, small ice pellets that fall from the sky.

5 ARIN is _____, which are drops of water falling to the earth.

6 NSWO is _____, which forms inside clouds when the temperature is very cold.

7 CLSDOU is _____, which form in the sky from the moisture in the air.

8 IWND is _____, which is moving air.

Science • 1–2 © 2005 Creative Teaching Press

Name _____ Date _____

Dressing for the Weather

Weather and Seasons

Did you wear a jacket today? Or, is it hot outside? If you learn about the weather, you will know how to dress correctly. The weather tells us what to wear each day.

Look at what each person is wearing. Draw a line from each person to the matching weather.

Name _____ Date _____

Windy Weather

Weather and Seasons

The sun heats the air and makes it move. Moving air creates wind. When the air moves gently we call it a breeze. If the air moves faster, we call it wind.

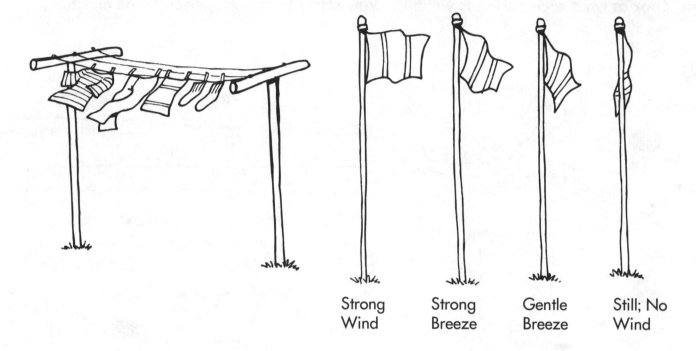

| Strong Wind | Strong Breeze | Gentle Breeze | Still; No Wind |

Draw an **X** over the picture that shows no wind. Circle the picture that shows a strong wind. Color the pictures that show a breeze blowing.

1   2   3   4

Name _____   Date _____

Stormy Weather

Weather and Seasons

There are several types of stormy weather. We call a strong snowstorm a **blizzard**. **Thunderstorms** have rain, thunder, and lightning. **Tornadoes** and **hurricanes** are storms that can cause a lot of damage.

What kind of stormy weather is shown in each picture?

tornado	blizzard	thunderstorm	hurricane

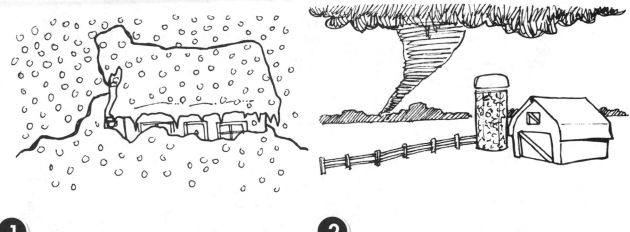

1 _____   **2** _____

3 _____   **4** _____

What Is Matter?

Matter

> The science term **matter** means anything that takes up space and weighs something. Some things take up a lot of space. Some things are very heavy. Other matter is small or lightweight.

1 Which has more matter? Circle it.

2 Which matter is the heaviest? Circle it.

3 Which matter takes up the least space? Circle it.

4 Which matter is the lightest? Circle it.

Name _____ Date _____

States of Matter

Matter

Matter comes in three forms or shapes. These are called the "states of matter." A **solid** has a definite size and shape. A **liquid** has a size (amount) but no shape of its own. A **gas** has no shape and no definite size.

Underline all the solid matter. Circle all the liquid matter. Color all the matter that is a gas.

Name _____ Date _____

Solids
Matter

All solids have their own shape and size. But all solids do not have the same shape or size. Some solids are very hard. Other solids can break easily.

Put a ✔ by the solids that have a round shape. Underline the solids that can break easily. Circle the solids that are very hard. Some solids can have more than one property.

baseball

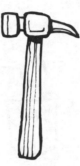

hammer

glass

chalk

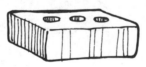

brick

rock

marble

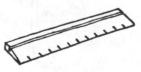

wood

cookie

Follow That Drop

Matter

Water is a useful liquid. Water can change from a liquid to a solid. It can change from a liquid to a gas. Water can be all three states of matter.

Fill in the blanks to show which state of matter the water is in. You will use the words in the box more than one time.

solid	liquid	gas

1 _____

2 _____

3 _____

4 _____

5 _____

6 _____

Lots of Air

Matter

Air is a gas. It is really a mixture of different gases. Air has no shape or size. The air spreads out to fill up the space it is in.

Look at the pictures. Read each statement. Write **T** if the statement is true or **F** if it is false.

1 _____ Air will spread out to fill up the space it is in.

2 _____ Air always has a round shape.

3 _____ Air is a mixture of gases.

4 _____ A gas has no shape or size.

5 _____ Air is usually invisible.

6 _____ Air is not made of matter.

Science • 1–2 © 2005 Creative Teaching Press

Name _____ Date _____

Sinking and Floating

Matter

> Some matter sinks in water. Other things float. Big things do not always sink. Small things do not always float. If an object is not too heavy for its size, it will float.

Write **sink** or **float** under each object to show what will happen if you put it in water.

1 _____

2 _____

3 _____

4 _____

5 _____

6 _____

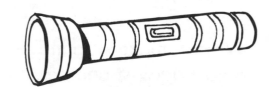

7 _____

Name _____   Date _____

Sound Vibrations

Sound

Sound is made when something wiggles or jiggles. We say it vibrates. These vibrations can travel through the air, water, or even the ground. We hear the sound when the vibrations reach our ears.

Four Ways to Make Sound

Use the words in the box to complete each sentence.

| plucking | blowing | stroking | striking | vibrates |

1 When an object _____ it makes a sound.

2 We can make a sound by hitting or _____ something.

3 We can make a sound by rubbing or _____ one object against another.

4 If we pick at something with our finger to make a sound, that is called _____.

5 A whistle makes a sound because we are _____ air through it.

Turn Up the Volume

Sound

Volume tells us how loud or soft a sound is. Volume is how far something moves back and forth as it vibrates. The bigger the vibration, the louder the sound.

Write **loud** or **soft** under each picture to describe its volume.

1 _____

2 _____

3 _____

4 _____

5 _____

6 _____

7 _____

8 _____

9 _____

What Is Pitch?

Sound

> **Pitch** tells us how high or low a note or sound is. The faster something vibrates, the higher the sound. Small objects vibrate faster than long, large objects. Small objects have a higher pitch.

Write **high** or **low** under each picture to describe the pitch of the sound.

1 _____
fog horn

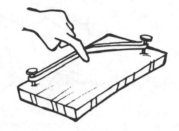

2 _____
large rubber band

3 _____
bird chirping

4 _____
fire engine siren

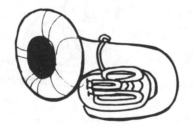

5 _____
tuba

6 _____
small glass

7 _____
whistle

8 _____
short end of a ruler

Name _____ Date _____

Musical Sounds

Sound

Musical sounds are made the same ways we make other sounds. Something has to vibrate. We can blow into, pluck, stroke, or strike an instrument. Then we hear the sound it makes.

Write under each musical instrument the way it makes a sound. You will use the words from the box more than one time.

blowing	striking	stroking	plucking

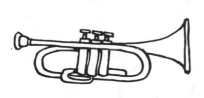

1 _____ **2** _____ **3** _____
Trumpet   Harp   Saxophone

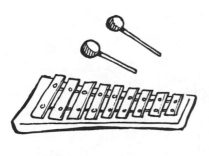

4 _____ **5** _____ **6** _____
Xylophone   Violin   Drum

Name _____ Date _____

Animal Sounds

Sound

Many animals make sounds. They can be loud or soft. Birds make high-pitched sounds. An elephant makes a low-pitched sound.

Look at the pictures. Read each statement. Write **T** if the statement is true or **F** if it is false.

1 _____ An elephant makes a loud sound.

2 _____ A cow makes a low-pitched "moo" sound.

3 _____ A mouse makes a high-pitched, soft sound.

4 _____ A lion's roar is a soft sound.

5 _____ The croak of a frog is a high-pitched sound.

6 _____ A cricket makes a chirping sound.

7 _____ A cat's meow is a high-pitched sound.

8 _____ A duck makes a buzzing sound.

Name _____ Date _____

Sound Travels

Sound

Sound travels in all directions. You can hear things in front of you, behind you, or even off to the side. The closer you are to a sound, the louder it seems.

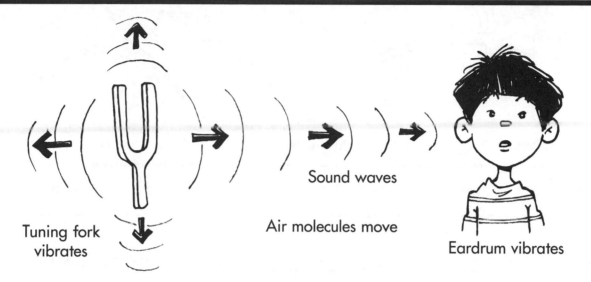

Tuning fork
vibrates

Sound waves

Air molecules move

Eardrum vibrates

Use the words in the box to complete each sentence.

travels	vibrations	side	louder	softer	ears

1 Our _____ pick up sounds that travel through the air.

2 When you are close to what makes a sound it sounds _____.

3 Sound _____ in all directions.

4 If you are far away from a sound, it sounds _____.

5 When the sound _____ reach our ears we hear.

6 We can hear in front or behind us, or even off to the _____.

Science • 1–2 © 2005 Creative Teaching Press

Puzzling Sounds

Sound

Unscramble the words and complete the sentences. Use the word box if you need help.

volume	pitch	loud	vibration	noise	echo	sound

1 HCTIP is _____, how high or low a sound is.

2 BIVIOTARN is _____, the movement back and forth that makes a sound.

3 LUVOEM is _____, the loudness of a sound.

4 OUSDN is _____, what we hear when something vibrates.

5 NESIO is _____, what we call sounds we do not like that bother us.

6 OECH is _____, a reflected sound that bounces back to us.

7 OLUD is _____, a sound that is NOT soft.

Shadows

Light and Shadows

When you block the light from the sun you cause a shadow to form. When the sun is low in the sky you have a long shadow. When the sun is over your head you have a small shadow.

Look at the pictures. Read each statement. Write **T** if the statement is true or **F** if it is false.

1 _____ You make shadows during the day.

2 _____ You have a small shadow in the morning.

3 _____ A shadow forms when something blocks the light.

4 _____ You have a long shadow in the afternoon.

5 _____ Your shadow always faces away from the sun.

6 _____ Only people can make shadows.

Name _____ Date _____

Rainbows

Light and Shadows

> Sunlight is made of all the colors of the rainbow. After it rains, sunlight passes through tiny drops of water in the air. This makes the colors separate. Then we see a rainbow.

Look at the picture of the rainbow. Read each statement. Write **T** if the statement is true or **F** if it is false.

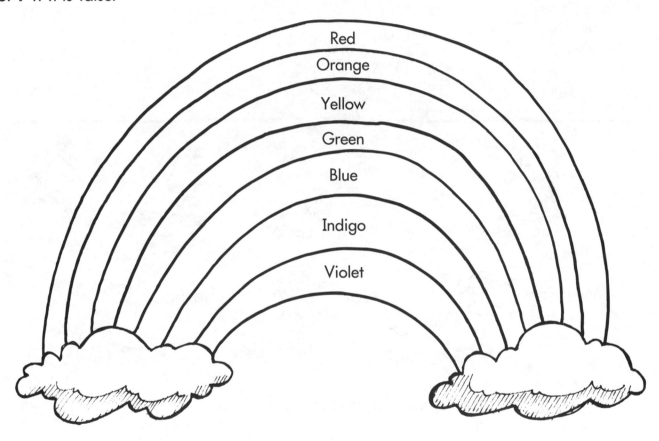

Red
Orange
Yellow
Green
Blue
Indigo
Violet

1 _____ The rainbow has six colors in it.

2 _____ Sunlight can make a rainbow after it rains.

3 _____ Sunlight is made of many colors.

4 _____ We always see orange at the top of the rainbow.

5 _____ The colors of light separate when they pass through a raindrop.

Safety in the Sun

Light and Shadows

There is a part of sunlight we cannot see. It is called ultraviolet light (UV). UV light can give you a sunburn, or cause skin cancer. It is important to protect yourself from this harmful part of the sunlight.

Wear a hat.

Wear sunglasses.

Use sunscreen.

Play in the shade.

Use the sun safety tips to help you complete the sentences.

1 You should wear a _____ that protects your face, ears, and neck from the sun.

2 Rub _____ on your skin to block the UV light in the sunlight.

3 _____ protect your eyes from the harmful rays of the sun.

4 Whenever possible, play in the _____ to avoid too much sun.

Simple Machines Crossword Puzzle

Simple Machines

Machines help us finish our work faster. Some machines give us more strength or power. Then we can do something that would be very hard to do without the machine. Machines make our work easier.

Complete the crossword puzzle. Use the words in the box for help.

| pulley | lever | screw | yes | inclined plane | axle | wheel |

Across

1. a machine that holds a light switch
3. helps move things up and down, or across
4. helps pry up heavy things
7. rod between two wheels

Down

2. makes things roll easier
5. opposite of "no"
6. machine that is a slanted ramp

Name _____   Date _____

Some Machines Cut Things

Simple Machines

Some tools or machines we use help us cut things. The machine may be used in the kitchen, at school, or outside for building something. All of these machines make our work easier.

Look at each machine. Color the machines that cut things.

Machines Can Hold Things

Simple Machines

Small machines we can hold in our hand are often called **tools**. Many of these machines are used for holding things. The machine may hold something in place, grab and hold on to something, or hold things together.

Draw an **X** on all the machines that are used to hold things.

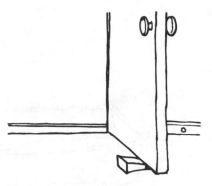

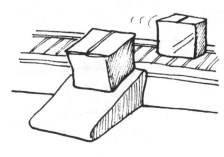

Machines Can Make Things Move

Simple Machines

Many machines make things move. We use some machines to make things go up or down, side to side, or even turn around. Machines can make things move forward or backward, too.

Look at each picture. Circle the arrows that show which way the machine makes something move.

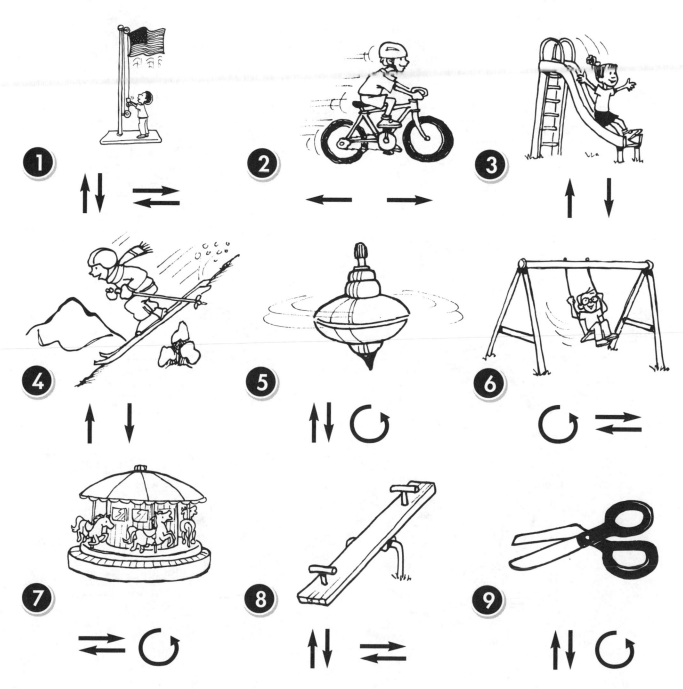

Name _____   Date _____

Which Machine Is Best?

Simple Machines

It is important to use the right machine for a job. That way the machine can help us do our work faster or more easily. If you use the wrong machine, you might get hurt or the work will be much harder.

Draw an **X** on all the pictures that show a machine being used the wrong way.

Machines at Home and School

Simple Machines

Machines help us to cook and clean at home. They help us work in the garden outside. At school we use machines to do our work every day. Can you think of some machines that you use?

Look at each picture. Find and circle four machines in each picture.

Machines at Home

Machines at School

Name _____   Date _____

What Is a Lever?

Simple Machines

A **lever** is one of the six simple machines. It is a bar or other long-shaped object that is used to move things. All levers have a **fulcrum**. This is the part of the lever that lets it move. Sometimes our hand is used for the fulcrum when we hold the machine.

Look at these tools. They all contain levers. Circle the two tools that have a fulcrum as part of the lever.

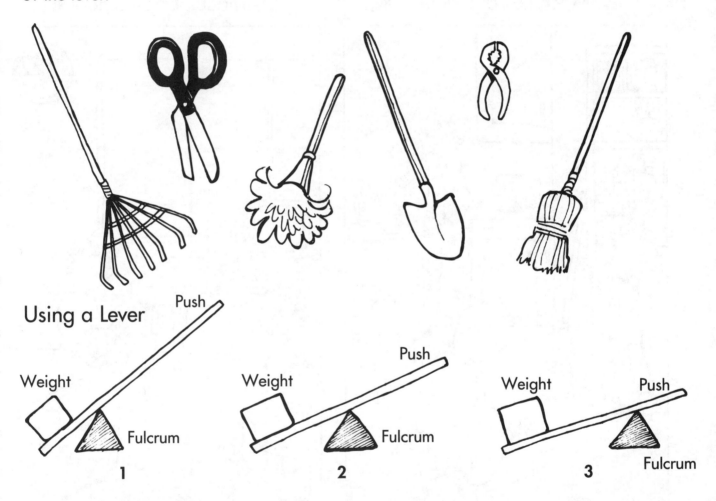

Using a Lever

Push

Weight   Fulcrum
1

Weight   Push   Fulcrum
2

Weight   Push   Fulcrum
3

Circle the correct answer.

1 A lever is easier to use when the fulcrum is (close to, far away from) the weight to be lifted.

2 This is shown in picture number _____.

Name _____   Date _____

Are These Screws?

Simple Machines

Many **screws** are used to hold things together. Screws can be used to cut holes in things, too. Other screws are used to lift things. A screw is one of the six simple machines.

Follow these steps to label the simple machines that contain screws:
1. Circle the parts of the machine that are screws.
2. If the screw is used for **holding** something, write **H** on the line.
3. If the screw is used to **cut** a hole in something, write **C** on the line.
4. If the screw is used for **lifting** something, write **L** on the line.

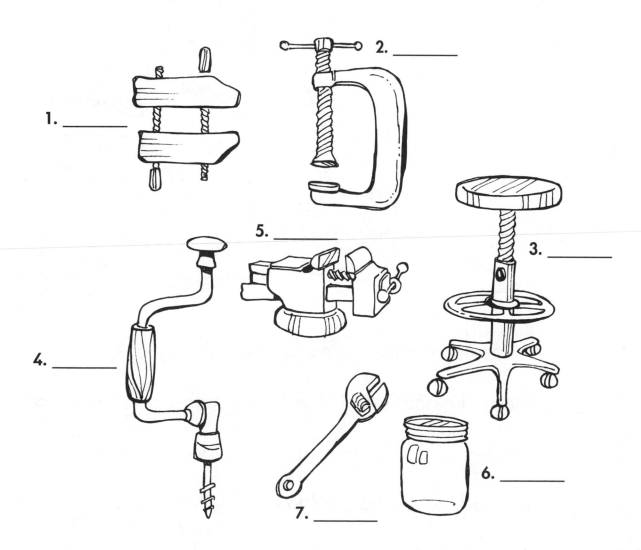

1. _____

2. _____

3. _____

4. _____

5. _____

6. _____

7. _____

Science • 1–2 © 2005 Creative Teaching Press

What Is an Inclined Plane?

Simple Machines

> An **inclined plane** is one of the six simple machines. An inclined plane is a slanted surface. It is also called a **ramp**. Inclined planes are used to move things to a higher or lower place more easily.

Look at all the inclined planes (ramps). Read each statement. Write **T** if the statement is true or **F** if it is false.

1 _____ A ramp is another name for an inclined plane.

2 _____ Inclined planes move objects to a higher or lower place.

3 _____ Ladders and stairs are examples of inclined planes.

4 _____ Inclined planes are used to move things across a flat floor.

5 _____ An inclined plane is a simple machine.

What Is a Wedge?

Simple Machines

A **wedge** is a simple machine made of one or two slanted surfaces. A wedge can be two inclined planes put together. Wedges can cut or split things apart. They can also hold things in place.

Follow these steps to label each wedge:
1. Circle the part of the machine that is a wedge.
2. If the wedge is for **holding** things in place, write an **H** on the line.
3. If the wedge is used to **cut** something, write **C** on the line.
4. If the wedge is used to **split** something apart, write **S** on the line.

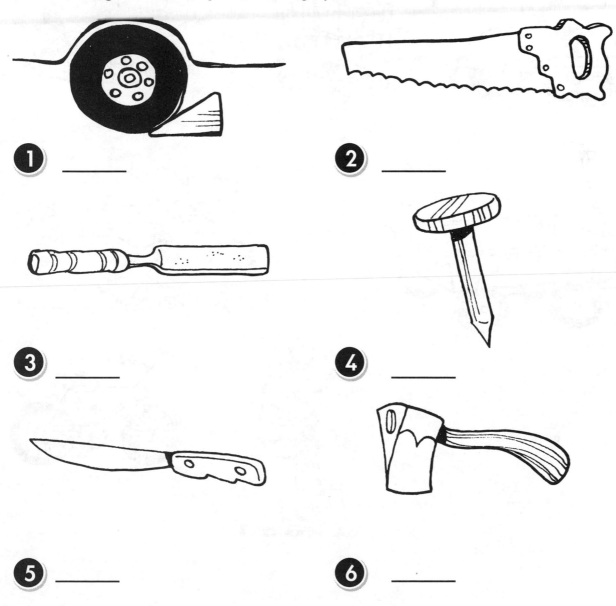

1 _____

2 _____

3 _____

4 _____

5 _____

6 _____

Name _____ Date _____

Wheels Are Useful Machines

Simple Machines

Wheels make things roll forward or backward or turn in place. A wheel is a simple machine that turns around a post called an **axle**. The axle may move with the wheel or separately. If the axle moves with the wheel, it gives us more force.

Color all of the wheels. Draw an **X** on the machines that do not have wheels.

How Does a Pulley Work?

Simple Machines

A **pulley** is a small wheel with a groove in it. A rope or cord fits in the groove and turns the pulley. Pulleys help move things up and down or side to side. Some pulleys are used to move objects that are hard to reach.

Circle all of the pulleys.

What Are Gears?

Simple Machines

Gears are wheels with teeth. The teeth are around the outer edges of the wheels. Gears turn in a circle to make a machine move. Gears can make a machine go faster or add more force to your effort.

Look at the picture. Read each statement. Write **T** if the statement is true or **F** if it is false.

1 _____ Gears are wheels with teeth.

2 _____ Gears on a bicycle can make the bike go faster.

3 _____ Sometimes gears may be hidden inside of a machine.

4 _____ Gears move by sliding backwards.

5 _____ Some gears add more force to help you do harder work.

6 _____ Gears can be found in many machines.

Name _____ Date _____

Machines Help Us Play Sports
Simple Machines

There are six simple machines: the lever, inclined plane, wedge, screw, wheel and axle, and pulley. Machines are not only used to make work easier for people. Some of them help us play sports.

Name the simple machine being used in each picture.

lever	wedge	wheel and axle

1 _____   **2** _____   **3** _____

4 _____   **5** _____   **6** _____

Magnets

Magnets

> A **magnet** is a piece of metal. It is made of iron or steel. A magnet can pick up things. It cannot pick up everything. Magnets can pick up things made of iron or steel.

Which objects will a magnet pick up? Circle them.

1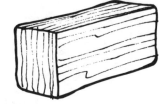

2

3

4

5

6

7

8

9

Name _____ Date _____

What Is a Magnetic Field?

Magnets

We cannot see how a magnet works. Its energy is invisible. This invisible energy is called a **magnetic field**. The magnetic field surrounds the magnet. It is strongest at the ends of a magnet.

Use the words in the box to complete each sentence.

can	cannot	ends	field

1 The energy of a magnet is strongest at the _____.

2 Around a magnet is a magnetic _____.

3 You _____ see a magnet.

4 You _____ see a magnetic field.

Name _____ Date _____

Magnets Have Poles

Magnets

The ends of a magnet are called the **poles**. They are named the **north** and **south** **poles**. Two magnets placed next to each other can do interesting things. Two like poles always repel, or push away, from each other. Unlike, or opposite poles, always attract each other.

Color the poles of the magnet.

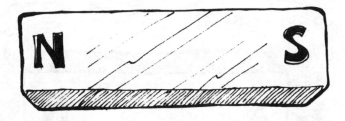

Draw arrows between each set of magnets to show how the poles would act when they come together.

attract   repel

Magnet Puzzle

Magnets

Find the letters that spell **MAGNET**. Color them brown. Color all the other letters orange.
What is hiding in the puzzle?

Magnets Come in Many Shapes

Magnets

> Magnets come in many shapes. Some are flat bars. Others are shaped like the letter U, or a horseshoe. Some magnets are shaped like rods, buttons, or rings.

Use the words in the box to label the magnet shapes.

horseshoe	rod	bar	ring	U-shape	button

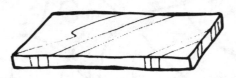

1 _____

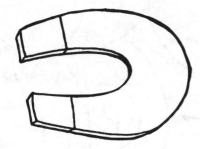

2 _____

3 _____

4 _____

5 _____

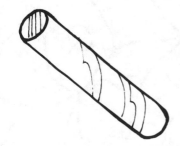

6 _____

Science • 1–2 © 2005 Creative Teaching Press

Answer Key

Animal Homes (page 5)

1. bird—nest
2. snake—under rocks
3. bee—hive/nest
4. bear—cave
5. rabbit—tall grass (some types live underground)
6. fish—water
7. squirrel—hole in tree
8. ants—underground

Lite under the Ground (page 6)

The following should be circled: ant, some rabbits, mole, some snakes, earthworm, and prairie dog.

Life in a Tree (page 7)

1. F
2. T
3. T
4. F
5. T
6. T

Life in a Pond (page 8)

1. B
2. C
3. E
4. D
5. A
6. F

Life in the Ocean (page 9)

I found <u>seaweed and a sea horse</u> hiding in the water.

Life in a Forest (page 10)

1. bear
2. birds
3. squirrel
4. fox
5. rabbit

Animal Pets (page 11)

Pictures and sentences will vary.

Plant Parts (page 12)

1. flower
2. stem
3. soil
4. leaf
5. roots

Plant Roots (page 13)

1. ground
2. food
3. water, minerals
4. carrot
5. hold
6. bean

Plant Stems (page 14)

1. daisy, tree
2. celery, tubes
3. onion
4. vines

Plant Leaves (page 15)

1. sun
2. air
3. jasmine
4. rose
5. maple
6. grass

Plant Seeds (page 16)

1. T
2. F
3. T
4. F
5. T
6. T

Plants Make Flowers (page 17)

```
Z  R  O  S  E  A  B  N  O
C  A  R  N  A  T  I  O  N
B  S  A  V  C  D  Y  D  E
R  G  L  I  L  A  B  S  P
V  F  H  X  O  I  J  I  T
P  O  P  P  Y  S  K  R  U
W  H  F  M  A  Y  L  I  L
I  J  L  O  W  X  O  P  I
X  P  E  T  U  N  I  A  P
U  A  U  E  U  T  C  I  L
K  N  L  E  R  D  E  Z  T
A  S  T  E  R  M  O  A  B
L  Y  U  T  N  A  K  C  R
```

How Plants Grow (page 18)

First row—color the last picture.

Second row—color the middle picture.

Third row—color the first picture.

Fourth row—color the last picture.

Plant Parts We Eat (page 19)

Roots—carrot, beet

Stems—asparagus, celery

Leaves—lettuce, spinach

Flowers—broccoli, cauliflower

Fruits—watermelon, pear

Seeds—corn, peanut

Tree Families (page 20)

1. E
2. H
3. E
4. E
5. H
6. E

Trees Are Useful (page 21)

The following should be colored: the newspaper, pencil, apple, cardboard box, and wooden chair.

My Eyes (page 22)

1. eyelashes
2. iris
3. pupil
4. white part
5. lens
6. tears

My Ears (page 23)

The following should be circled: the whistle, thundercloud, baby crying, bee, alarm clock, dog barking, radio, and telephone.

How Does It Taste? (page 24)

Sour—lines from the grapefruit and the lemon

Sweet—lines from the strawberry and the ice-cream cone

Bitter—lines from the coffee and the aspirin

Salty—lines from the potato chips and the pretzel

How Does It Smell? (page 25)

The following should be circled: flower, chocolate bar, perfume, strawberry, bread, and popcorn.

The following should be underlined: dirty socks, garbage can, and skunk.

Sense of Touch (page 26)

Pain—color the finger.

Smooth—color the mirror.

Cold—color the ice cube.

Hard—color the baseball.

Soft—color the pillow.

Healthy Eating (page 27)

1. vegetables
2. 2 to 3
3. meats, beans, and nuts
4. fruits
5. breads and grains
6. extras

Fruits and Vegetables (page 28)

1. fruit
2. fruit
3. vegetable
4. fruit
5. vegetable
6. fruit
7. fruit
8. vegetable
9. fruit

Body Word Scramble (page 29)

1. bones
2. heart
3. nose
4. brain
5. skin
6. lungs
7. eyes
8. ears
9. tongue

Insects (page 30)

1. T
2. F
3. T
4. F
5. F
6. T
7. T
8. T

Insect Metamorphosis (page 31)

1. eggs
2. nymphs
3. metamorphosis
4. larva
5. pupa
6. adult

Amphibians (page 32)

1. eggs
2. tadpoles
3. gills
4. legs
5. lungs
6. frogs

Reptiles (page 33)

The following should be circled: the lizard, alligator, snake, and turtle.

Fish (page 34)

1. T
2. T
3. T
4. T
5. T
6. T

Birds (page 35)

1. mud
2. hole
3. round
4. barn
5. hanging

Mammals (page 36)

1. Circle the dolphin.
2. Underline the rabbit.
3. Draw an X on the cow.
4. Color the dog yellow.
5. Draw a box around the elephant.
6. Color the bat brown.

What's on the Outside of an Animal's Body? (page 37)

1. Underline the owl and duck.
2. Circle the frog and earthworm.
3. Color the duck, fox, and owl.
4. Draw a box around the lizard and fish.
5. Draw an X on the crab and snail.

Colorful Animals (page 38)

Blue—mouse and raccoon

Green—duck and heron

Yellow—two fish

Red—turtle and snake

Purple—butterfly, ant, caterpillar, and dragonfly

Orange—frog and tadpoles

What Animals Eat (page 39)

1. T
2. T
3. F
4. T
5. T
6. F

How Animals Move (page 40)

1. fish or frog
2. rabbit or frog
3. bird
4. snake
5. caterpillar

Animals of Long Ago (page 41)

1. b
2. c
3. d
4. a

Dinosaur Lunch (page 42)

1. F
2. F
3. T
4. T
5. T

Dinosaur Footprints (page 43)

1. Footprint #1
2. Footprint #3
3. Footprint #2
4. Footprint #2
5. Footprint #1 or #3

Dinosaur Puzzle (page 44)

The dinosaur in the puzzle is a Tyrannosaurus.

What Is Soil? (page 45)

1. water
2. rocks
3. sand
4. plants
5. animals
6. soil

What Is a Rock? (page 46)

1. Circle 1, 2, 3, 9
2. Underline 5, 6
3. Place a check by 1, 2, 5, 7, 8
4. Draw a box around 3, 4, 6, 9, 10

Why Don't Rocks Last Forever? (page 47)

1. wind
2. earthquake
3. water
4. ice

What Do People Do with Rocks? (page 48)

1. house
2. dam
3. decoration
4. road

Rocks Have Hidden Treasures (page 49)

The following should be colored: the soda can, scissors, penny, and aluminum foil.

Some Rocks Are Pretty (page 50)

1. T
2. F
3. T
4. T
5. T
6. T

Rocks from Long Ago (page 51)

1. earth
2. deep
3. age
4. tools
5. dig

Over Hill and Dale—Landforms (page 52)

1. plain
2. mountain
3. cliff
4. canyon
5. valley
6. hill

Earth Crossword Puzzle (page 53)

Across

1. mountain
2. rocks
3. soil

Down

1. mud
3. sand
4. island
5. water
6. hill

Earth's Natural Resources (page 54)

The following should have a ✓: air and sun, land, trees, water, ocean, and oil.

What Wastes Natural Resources? (page 55)

1. Draw an X through the picture on the right.
2. Draw an X through the picture on the right.
3. Draw an X through the picture on the left.
4. Draw an X through the picture on the left.

What Is Smog? (page 56)

1. T
2. T
3. F
4. T
5. F
6. T

How We Use Water (page 57)

1. daily living
2. fun
3. daily living
4. work
5. daily living
6. work
7. fun
8. daily living
9. fun

Help Save Our Water (page 58)

Circle any four of these: the girl hosing down the drive-way, the hose running by the car being washed, the sprinkler, and the dripping faucets.

Saving Energy at Home (page 59)

Color any five of these: refrigerator door left open, radio left on in bedroom, wasting hot water in bathroom, faucet left running in the kitchen, TV left on, and outdoor light left on.

What Saves Paper? (page 60)

The following should have a ✓: 1, 3, 4, 6.

How We Use Air (page 61)

1. make things work
2. make things work
3. dry things
4. for fun
5. make things work
6. for fun
7. make things work
8. dry things
9. make things work (or for fun)

Where on Earth Does Our Food Come From? (page 62)

1. chickens
2. cows, lambs
3. trees
4. farms
5. fish
6. milk

Where Does Our Water Come From? (page 63)

1. F
2. T
3. T
4. T
5. T
6. T
7. T

Where Does Fuel Come From? (page 64)

1. wood
2. natural gas
3. oil
4. gasoline
5. coal
6. diesel

What Are Our Clothes Made From? (page 65)

Cotton plant—T-shirt

Silkworm—silk scarf

Flax plant—linen tablecloth

Sheep—wool sweater

Cows—leather shoes

The Sun (page 66)

1. star
2. bright
3. gases
4. light
5. closest
6. hot

Day and Night (page 67)

1. twenty-four
2. warmer
3. colder
4. rotates
5. day
6. night

The Moon (page 68)

1. F
2. T
3. F
4. T
5. T
6. T

Starry Night (page 69)

1. Little
2. Big
3. constellations
4. Belt
5. dog

Cloudy Day (page 70)

1. cirrus
2. cumulonimbus
3. cumulus
4. stratus

Drawings should resemble the samples.

Sunny Day (page 71)

1. T
2. T
3. F
4. T
5. T

Is it Going to Rain? (page 72)

1. moisture
2. dark
3. air
4. clouds
5. rain

What's the Temperature? (page 73)

1. C
2. B
3. A
4. C
5. A

The Four Seasons (page 74)

1. spring
2. winter
3. autumn
4. summer
5. winter
6. autumn
7. spring
8. summer

What's Falling Out of the Sky—Precipitation (page 75)

1. snow—Soft crystals or flakes of ice formed in clouds when the temperature falls below freezing.
2. rain—Drops of water that fall to the ground.
3. hail—Small round pieces of ice that fall like rain. They form during summer thunderstorms.
4. sleet—Frozen or partly frozen rain.

Weather Word Scramble (page 76)

1. fog
2. lightning
3. thunder
4. hail
5. rain
6. snow
7. clouds
8. wind

Dressing for the Weather (page 77)

1. sunny weather
2. rainy weather
3. snowy weather
4. windy weather

Windy Weather (page 78)

1. Color
2. Draw an X
3. Color
4. Circle

Stormy Weather (page 79)

1. blizzard
2. tornado
3. thunderstorm
4. hurricane

What Is Matter? (page 80)

1. Circle the TV.

2. Circle the airplane.

3. Circle the pencil.

4. Circle the balloon.

States of Matter (page 81)

Underline 3, 5, 7, 9.

Circle 2, 4, 8.

Color 1 and 6.

Solids (page 82)

Put a ✔ by the baseball and marble. Underline the chalk, glass, and cookie. Color the baseball, hammer, brick, rock, marble, and wood.

Follow That Drop (page 83)

1. solid

2. liquid and gas

3. solid

4. gas

5. liquid

6. liquid

Lots of Air (page 84)

1. T

2. F

3. T

4. T

5. T

6. F

Sinking and Floating (page 85)

1. sink

2. float

3. sink

4. float

5. sink

6. float

7. sink

Sound Vibrations (page 86)

1. vibrates

2. striking

3. stroking

4. plucking

5. blowing

Turn Up the Volume (page 87)

1. soft

2. loud

3. loud

4. loud

5. soft

6. loud

7. soft

8. loud

9. soft

What Is Pitch? (page 88)

1. low
2. low
3. high
4. high
5. low
6. high
7. high
8. high

Musical Sounds (page 89)

1. blowing
2. plucking
3. blowing
4. striking
5. stroking
6. striking

Animal Sounds (page 90)

1. T
2. T
3. T
4. F
5. F
6. T
7. T
8. F

Sound Travels (page 91)

1. ears
2. louder
3. travels
4. softer
5. vibrations
6. side

Puzzling Sounds (page 92)

1. pitch
2. vibration
3. volume
4. sound
5. noise
6. echo
7. loud

Shadows (page 93)

1. T
2. F
3. T
4. T
5. T
6. F

Rainbows (page 94)

1. F
2. T
3. T
4. F
5. T

Safety in the Sun (page 95)

1. hat

2. sunscreen

3. sunglasses

4. shade

Simple Machines Crossword Puzzle (page 96)

Across

1. screw

3. pulley

4. lever

7. axle

Down

2. wheel

5. yes

6. inclined plane

Some Machines Cut Things (page 97)

The following should be colored: the knife, saw, scissors, and axe.

Machines Can Hold Things (page 98)

Draw an X on 1, 2, 3, 5, 9.

Machines Can Make Things Move (page 99)

1. Circle up and down arrows

2. Circle arrow to the right

3. Circle down arrow

4. Circle down arrow

5. Circle turning around arrow

6. Circle back and forth arrows

7. Circle turning around arrow

8. Circle up and down arrows

9. Circle up and down arrows

Which Machine Is Best? (page 100)

Draw an X on 1, 3, 4, 5.

Machines at Home and School (page 101)

Home—circle the broom, vacuum, coffee maker, and iron (can include the ironing board). Note: Some children may circle the hinges on the cabinet doors. School—circle the clock, projector, pencil and pencil sharpener, and computer.

What Is a Lever? (page 102)

Circle the scissors and the pliers.

1. close to   2. 1

Are These Screws? (page 103)

1. H

2. H

3. L

4. C

5. H

6. H

7. H

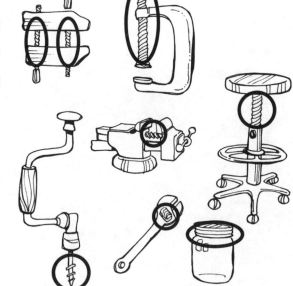

What Is an Inclined Plane? (page 104)

1. T
2. T
3. T
4. F
5. T

What Is a Wedge? (page 105)

1. H
2. C
3. C
4. H
5. C
6. S

Wheels Are Useful Machines (page 106)

The following should be colored: the wheels of the roller skates, the grocery cart, the pizza cutter wheel, the wagon wheels, the reel part of the fishing rod, and the wheels of the bicycle.

Draw an X on the ice skates and shovel.

How Does a Pulley Work? (page 107)

What Are Gears? (page 108)

1. T
2. T
3. T
4. F
5. T
6. T

Machines Help Us Play Sports (page 109)

1. lever
2. wedge
3. wheel and axle
4. wedge
5. wheel and axle
6. lever

Magnets (page 110)

Circle 1, 2, 5, 6, 9.

What Is a Magnetic Field? (page 111)

1. ends

2. field

3. can

4. cannot

Magnets Have Poles (page 112)

Color the ends marked N and S.

1. Attracts; arrows go together

2. Repels; arrows push apart

3. Repels; arrows push apart

4. Attracts; arrows go together

Magnet Puzzle (page 113)

The puzzle shows a picture of a dog and a dog's bowl.

Magnets Come in Many Shapes (page 114)

1. bar

2. horseshoe

3. U-shape

4. button

5. ring

6. rod